Original title:
Navigating Friendships

Copyright © 2024 Swan Charm
All rights reserved.

Author: Kaido Väinamäe
ISBN HARDBACK: 978-9916-86-806-5
ISBN PAPERBACK: 978-9916-86-807-2
ISBN EBOOK: 978-9916-86-808-9

Anchors on Troubled Waters

In storms where shadows fall,
Our hearts become the call.
We stand on tempest's shore,
Anchored to love once more.

The waves may crash and roar,
Yet we will not lose score.
With eyes that pierce the night,
We find our guiding light.

Drifting on tides of fate,
Our souls will navigate.
Through waters deep and wide,
With hope we will abide.

Each challenge that we face,
Brings strength to our embrace.
Together we can grow,
Through all we come to know.

So here's to troubled seas,
To sailing with such ease.
In unity, we thrive,
Our anchors keep us alive.

The Map of Hearts Aligned

In pencil drawn with care,
Our dreams are written there.
Each line a whispered truth,
A guide in our own youth.

With time, we shift and sway,
But stars will light our way.
Through valleys deep and wide,
In faith, we will abide.

Connections forged in time,
With every heartbeat, rhyme.
Our journeys intertwine,
In patterns so divine.

Through mountains high we climb,
In rhythm and in rhyme.
The map unfolds anew,
As I wander to you.

With every step we take,
New paths that we will make.
In sync as days unfold,
Our hearts map love untold.

Places Where We Meet

In quiet corners, dreams,
Where sunlight softly beams.
With laughter in the air,
We find our solace there.

Beneath the ancient trees,
We sway with gentle breeze.
In whispers and in sighs,
We share our secret ties.

On cobblestone paths roam,
Feels just like coming home.
With every glance, we find,
The comfort intertwined.

Amidst the city's hum,
Where distant echoes come.
In chaos, we find peace,
Our love will never cease.

From dawn to evening's glow,
In every place we go.
Together, we create,
The moments that await.

The Bridge Between Us

Two souls entwined in gentle grace,
A bridge unites our sacred space.
Through storms and sunshine, hand in hand,
Together we weave, together we stand.

Whispers of love in the quiet night,
Guiding us home, a beacon of light.
No distance can dim what we hold dear,
In every heartbeat, you're always near.

With bridges built on trust and care,
Every challenge faced, together we dare.
In laughter and tears, we find our way,
Our bond, a love that will forever stay.

Seasons of Togetherness

Winter wraps us in a gentle fold,
With whispers of warmth and stories told.
Spring blooms bright with colors anew,
In every petal, I see me and you.

Summer's sun, in radiant glow,
Laughing together, letting time flow.
Autumn leaves dance, a joyous parade,
In every moment, memories made.

Each season brings its own sweet charm,
With open hearts, we stay warm.
Through changing tides, we grow and bend,
In every season, love knows no end.

Radiant Paths We Walk

Two paths converge, a journey begins,
With every step, our new world spins.
Through golden fields and shadowed lanes,
We craft our dreams, despite the rains.

In laughter's echo, we find our song,
With every heartbeat, where we belong.
Hand in hand, we face each dawn,
With courage strong, our fears are gone.

The trails we tread, both wild and free,
In every moment, just you and me.
A dance of fate, a whispered vow,
In radiant light, we embrace the now.

The Map of Hearts

In the compass of dreams, our hearts align,
Every mark a memory, so rare, divine.
With laughter as our guiding star,
We chart a course, no matter how far.

Each fold and crease tells tales unspoken,
Of love that's forged and never broken.
Through valleys low and mountains high,
Together we soar, our spirits fly.

The map unfolds with every glance,
In every heartbeat, there's a chance.
To navigate life with love as the guide,
In the map of hearts, forever side by side.

Wings of Encouragement

Lift your head, take a flight,
Trust your heart, embrace the light.
Every dream is worth the chase,
With each step, you'll find your place.

Through the storms, your spirit rise,
Believe in you, see through the lies.
With each breath, let courage breed,
You possess all that you need.

Let doubt vanish, let hopes glow,
For within you, strength will grow.
Spread your wings, let passions soar,
In your heart, there's so much more.

With every fall, you learn to stand,
Keep on working, hand in hand.
In the struggle, joy unveils,
Trust yourself, the heart prevails.

In this journey, take your flight,
Wings of courage, shining bright.
Together we will light the way,
For today is a brand-new day.

Shadows of Gentle Words

In the silence, whispers flow,
Gentle thoughts begin to grow.
Each kind word a soothing balm,
In the chaos, find your calm.

Speak with grace, let kindness reign,
Heal the heart, relieve the pain.
In the shadows, light can play,
Bringing hope to every day.

Words of comfort, soft and true,
Building bridges, me and you.
In every sentence, love takes flight,
Turning darkness into light.

Share your dreams and fears alike,
In this journey, we will hike.
Together in our quiet space,
Finding joy in every trace.

Let our voices intertwine,
In this bond, your soul is mine.
Through the storms and sunny skies,
Gentle words can lift us high.

The Canvas of Connection

Brushstrokes of our lives collide,
On this canvas, side by side.
Every color tells a tale,
In our hearts, we shall prevail.

Canvas stretches, wide and free,
Bringing out our harmony.
In the art of sharing time,
Every moment feels like rhyme.

With each line, a story shared,
In this space, we are both bared.
Trust the hues, let darkness fade,
In togetherness, we are made.

From the shadows, spark the light,
Every splatter, pure delight.
In this tapestry we weave,
Through connection, we believe.

Frame our memories, bright and bold,
As the years of life unfold.
Through every stroke, forever true,
The canvas shines with me and you.

The Journey of Shared Stories

Every story finds its voice,
In the sharing, we rejoice.
Each chapter penned, a life explored,
Through our hearts, we are adored.

Gather round and lend an ear,
In the laughter, ease the fear.
Tales of courage, pain, and grace,
In this journey, find your place.

From the pages of our past,
Lessons learned and shadows cast.
In the words, we're intertwined,
Together, peace we shall find.

With each tale, we heal, we grow,
Through the trials, let love flow.
Hand in hand, we write anew,
The journey holds me close to you.

A saga rich with hearts combined,
In our stories, we are aligned.
Bound by tales of joy and strife,
Together we embrace this life.

Twists and Turns of the Heart

In shadows deep where secrets lay,
The heart takes paths that pulse and sway.
With every twist, a lesson learned,
In every yearn, the fire burned.

We chase the echoes of a sigh,
In crowded rooms, two souls pass by.
Yet in the silence, hope can spark,
As love ignites from a tiny dark.

Each tear we shed a leaf released,
In winding roads, our fears decreased.
With open arms, the journey bends,
For every heartache, love transcends.

The compass points the way we go,
In circles round, the heart can know.
When whispers linger, softly heard,
We trust the map within one word.

So let us dance where stars collide,
In heart's embrace, our dreams abide.
Through twists and turns, we'll find our way,
In love's rich soil, our roots will stay.

Silences Between Us

In quiet rooms where shadows play,
Our hearts converse in soft ballet.
Each silent glance a secret shared,
In restful depths, we find we're paired.

What words might fail to capture true,
In silent vows, we start anew.
With thoughtful pauses, time expands,
An unspoken understanding stands.

The weight of moments, bittersweet,
In every sigh, our souls repeat.
A tender bond, though words are few,
In silences, I find your hue.

What dreams arise in whispered night,
Against the stars, our hopes take flight.
Between each beat, a tale unfolds,
In gentle warmth, our love grows bold.

With every breath, we linger near,
In silent strength, I feel you here.
Though worlds may change and time may bend,
In silence sweet, our hearts descend.

Compass Points of Compassion

When hearts are heavy, burdens shared,
A compass guides, your kindness bared.
Through storms and trials, hand in hand,
Compassion's light will help us stand.

Each gesture small can move a soul,
In gentle ways, we find our role.
With open minds, we seek to learn,
In love's embrace, our spirits turn.

From distant shores, we bring our gifts,
Through heavy tides, the heart uplifts.
Together here, we stand as one,
With hearts aligned until we're done.

As compass points shift in the night,
We find our path in love's pure light.
Through winding roads and skies unsure,
Our bonds of grace will hold us secure.

In every fray, we rise to soar,
Compassion's flame will evermore.
In unity, we write our fate,
With open hearts, we cultivate.

Footnotes of Loyalty

In whispered words, I find a guide,
Footnotes written where hearts abide.
With every promise gently made,
In loyalty, we won't evade.

Each memory holds a precious truth,
In laughter shared, a glimpse of youth.
Through trials faced and moments blessed,
Our steadfast bond will stand the test.

The pages turn, but we remain,
In joyful times and through the pain.
With every scar, a story told,
A testament to love we hold.

Together forged in fire and grace,
In every challenge, we find our place.
Through distances, our hearts entwine,
In footnotes of love, a sacred line.

So here we stand, both tried and true,
In every storm, I'll shelter you.
In loyalty's embrace, we thrive,
Forever woven, we are alive.

The Compass of Companionship

In the forest, friends unite,
Paths entwined, a joyful sight.
Through the trials, laughs we share,
Guiding light with love and care.

When storms rage and shadows fall,
Together we can stand so tall.
With every step, our bond does grow,
A compass true, we always know.

In silence shared, in whispers deep,
Promises made are ours to keep.
With every memory, we create,
A map of warmth to navigate.

Through valleys low and mountains high,
With trusted hearts, we touch the sky.
In every journey, hand in hand,
Together, always, we will stand.

Echoes of Shared Secrets

In twilight's hush, secrets unfold,
Whispers soft, stories told.
In sacred circles, truths we share,
Echoes linger, hearts laid bare.

Beneath the moon's watchful gaze,
We trace our hopes, our hidden ways.
With every laugh, every sigh,
Joy resounds as shadows fly.

The bonds we forge, unseen threads,
In laughter's warmth, love spreads.
Through trials faced and dreams we weave,
In trust we build, in hope we believe.

With every secret, deeper ties,
In friendship's glow, our spirit flies.
Together strong, we find our voice,
In echoes rich, we will rejoice.

Currents of Camaraderie

In rivers wide, our souls converge,
With every wave, our hearts emerge.
In laughter's flow, we set our sails,
Against the wind, through storms and gales.

A current strong of shared delight,
Together we stand, ready to fight.
With every challenge, hand in hand,
In unity, we make our stand.

Through swirling tides and shifting sands,
Side by side, we take our stands.
In deep waters, we dive and learn,
In every heartbeat, friendships burn.

With every twist, our lives entwined,
In camaraderie, love defined.
As waves may crash, we'll never fade,
Together, strong, our bond is made.

Under the Stars of Trust

Beneath the sky, where starlight gleams,
We share our hopes, our wildest dreams.
In every glance, a promise shines,
Together woven in cosmic lines.

With constellations as our guide,
We journey on this endless ride.
In twilight's calm, our fears laid bare,
In trust we find, there's strength to share.

Each twinkling star, a tale to weave,
In darkest nights, we believe.
With every wish upon the sky,
Together we soar, as dreams fly high.

In the warmth of night, our spirits dance,
Amidst the stars, we take our chance.
With trust as light, we'll light the way,
Under the spell of the Milky Way.

The Compass of Connection

In the heart where friendships dwell,
Moments shared, we weave our spell.
With every smile and every tear,
We find our way, we feel you near.

Guiding lights that brightly shine,
Mapping paths, our souls entwine.
Through every storm and sunny day,
Our compass points, we'll find our way.

With whispered dreams that softly rise,
In laughter's echo, we touch the skies.
Together we stand, our spirits blend,
In this journey, love knows no end.

Through winding roads and trails unknown,
In every heart, a seed is sown.
The compass spins, but we won't stray,
In unity, we'll find our way.

So hand in hand, in step we move,
With every moment, we will prove.
That in this dance, so rich and grand,
Connection's compass holds our hand.

Chasing Stars in Our Circle

Beneath the sky of endless night,
We gather close, our hearts alight.
With dreams like stars, we take our chance,
In this circle, our souls enhance.

Each twinkle whispers tales anew,
In every glance, a wish comes true.
Together we soar, reaching high,
Chasing stars as they drift by.

In laughter shared and stories spun,
Each moment shines, a treasured one.
With every heartbeat, we'll ignite,
The magic found in shared delight.

Through challenges faced, we will stand,
With open hearts, we join the band.
Our circle tight, our spirits leap,
In chasing stars, our bond runs deep.

As constellations grace the skies,
We'll find our strength where love complies.
Together, we'll paint the night divine,
Chasing stars, our paths align.

Threads Woven in Laughter

In the tapestry of joyful days,
Laughter weaves in so many ways.
Each chuckle brightens up the room,
A bond that flourishes, blooms in bloom.

With every joke and playful jest,
We find our solace, we feel our best.
These threads connect, they intertwine,
In warmth and joy, our hearts align.

Through whispered secrets and shared dreams,
In laughter's glow, our spirit gleams.
A symphony of joyous sound,
In each embrace, our love is found.

So let us dance in joyous cheer,
And weave the moments we hold dear.
For every laugh, a memory stays,
In threads of laughter, love always plays.

As time moves on, we'll carry forth,
The joy we share, our endless worth.
Together, we'll craft a world of glee,
In laughter's embrace, we are set free.

Echoes of Shared Secrets

In the quiet, secrets blend,
Whispers shared, a bond to mend.
With every word, a trust bestowed,
In the depths of hearts, they flowed.

Echoes linger in the night,
Holding truth within our sight.
With every secret softly told,
A treasure found, a hand to hold.

Through twists and turns, we navigate,
In each confession, we create.
The shadows dance, a sacred space,
In echoes past, we find our grace.

So gather near, let silence speak,
In shared secrets, we are unique.
Each story woven, a sacred pact,
In these echoes, we'll never lack.

As time reveals what once was hid,
Our hearts unlock, the truth amid.
In every echo, love reassures,
Together we stand, our bond endures.

Reflections in Shared Silence

In twilight's hush, we sit so still,
With whispered thoughts, our hearts to fill.
Time drifts gently, a soft embrace,
In silence shared, we find our place.

Memories dance like shadows cast,
Each one a story, an echo of the past.
Together we breathe, without a need,
For words that fade, like fallen seed.

Eyes meet softly, a tender glance,
In this quiet moment, we take a chance.
Layers unfold, like petals bloom,
Within the silence, hearts consume.

The world outside may rush and roam,
But here, in stillness, we find our home.
Life slows down, in this sacred space,
Reflections linger, an endless grace.

Journeys Through Laughter

With every chuckle, joy takes flight,
In sparkling eyes, the world feels bright.
We wander paths where smiles ignite,
Together we dance, from day to night.

Each laugh a treasure, a story to share,
Light as a feather, we float through air.
Moments of joy, so pure, so sweet,
With laughter as music, we skip to the beat.

The road may twist, the clouds may chime,
In laughter's embrace, we make our time.
Let go of worries, let tomorrow wait,
In joy's warm hold, we create our fate.

From silly jokes to tales of woe,
We heal each other, let laughter flow.
In every giggle, a bond we weave,
Through journeys of joy, we learn to believe.

The Heart's Compass

In the quiet of night, we pause and dream,
The heart whispers softly, a gentle theme.
A compass points true, in shadows and light,
Guiding us home through the darkest night.

Each beat a promise, a call to the soul,
Mapping the moments that make us whole.
In love's sweet embrace, we find our way,
Through valleys low and mountains gray.

The north star gleams, a beacon so bright,
In searches of truth, it shines with might.
The heart knows where wanderers roam,
In every step, it leads us home.

Through storms of doubt and winds of change,
The heart's compass holds, steadfast and strange.
With each new dawn, we rise and embrace,
The journey of life, with hope's warm grace.

Whispers of Resilience

In whispered winds, the stories flow,
Of struggles faced and seeds we sow.
Through trials we bend, yet never break,
Resilience blooms with each step we take.

Life's gentle hands, they shape and mold,
In the heat of fire, our spirits unfold.
Every setback, a lesson learned,
In the heart's forge, our courage burned.

Soft whispers echo, "You can be strong,"
Guiding us gently when everything feels wrong.
For in the shadows, we find our might,
In whispers of resilience, we ignite.

With every heartbeat, we rise anew,
Embracing the journey, our dreams in view.
Together we stand, in hope we trust,
For in each challenge, we find our just.

Voices Carried on the Wind

Whispers float on gentle breeze,
Secrets shared among the trees.
Songs of old from faraway,
Echo softly, night and day.

Carried forth on currents wide,
Hopes and dreams refuse to hide.
Every note a tale of lore,
Finding peace upon the shore.

In the stillness, hear them call,
Unity that binds us all.
Voices rise, the world alive,
In their harmony, we thrive.

Journeys Across Uncharted Waters

Waves crash down, horizons blur,
Nautical maps, the heart will stir.
Every ripple tells a tale,
Of brave souls who dared to sail.

Stars above, the guiding lights,
Charting paths through endless nights.
In the distance, whispers grow,
Of lands unseen and dreams below.

Taste the salt, feel the spray,
Oceans wide, lead the way.
Journeys start from shores unknown,
In each wave, a seed is sown.

The Golden Thread of Understanding

Woven tight, a tapestry,
Threads connect in harmony.
With each stitch, a story told,
In colors bright, and shades of gold.

Listening hearts begin to see,
Bonds that build community.
Through the fabric, wisdom flows,
In every corner, kindness grows.

Compassion blooms, bright and true,
Intertwined, me and you.
Together we can weave a dream,
On this thread, we all shall gleam.

Lanterns in Each Other's Night

In the dark, a flicker shines,
Guiding paths, gentle signs.
Lanterns held with hands outspread,
Illuminating words unsaid.

Through the gloom, our spirits dance,
Each soft glow, a fleeting chance.
Together facing shadows deep,
In this light, our secrets keep.

When the storm clouds loom above,
We share light, and lift with love.
Each lantern lit, a bond we forge,
In the night, our hopes emerge.

The Art of Listening

In silence we find the softest sound,
A whisper of thoughts, intricately bound.
Ears open wide, hearts patiently wait,
For stories unfolding, a shared fate.

Eyes that glisten with every note,
Capturing feelings, as words float.
The pause that breathes in between lines,
Crafts a connection that softly aligns.

Listening deeply, we learn to see,
The beauty of voices, both you and me.
With every heartbeat, a new truth shines,
In the art of listening, the soul intertwines.

Footprints on the Path

Each step we take, a mark in the sand,
Footprints together, hand in hand.
Through fields of joy, and trails of strife,
We walk this journey, carving life.

The echoes of laughter in warm sunlight,
Guide us through shadows, illuminating night.
With every stumble, we learn to rise,
Finding strength in our shared skies.

Waters may swirl, and storms may roar,
But side by side, we'll always explore.
These footprints linger, a story to tell,
On this winding path, we know it well.

Shadows of Shared Moments

In quiet corners, shadows play,
Remnants of laughter, love on display.
Reverberating whispers of days gone by,
Memories linger, as moments fly.

Each smile captured, a flicker of light,
Through swirling dusk and the softening night.
A shared glance speaks when words take flight,
In the shadows, we find our delight.

Together we weave this tapestry bright,
Each thread a story, in day or in night.
In shadows we dance, as time gently bends,
Creating a haven where love never ends.

The Dance of Disagreement

Two minds in motion, a delicate sway,
A dance of words, in night and in day.
Each step uncertain, but grounded in trust,
Finding harmony, even in dust.

A clash of opinions, like thunder in air,
Yet in the storm, there lies a flair.
Through passion and fire, we challenge the night,
In the dance of disagreement, we seek the light.

With patience we pivot, we listen, we turn,
From embers of conflict, new bridges we learn.
In every debate, respect is our guide,
In this dance of discord, we flourish, collide.

The Compass of Experience

In the quiet of the night, we seek,
The stars that guide our lost hearts' beat.
Each trial, a lesson, carved in stone,
With every step, we find our own.

Winds of change may bend our way,
Yet spring will follow winter's gray.
Through storms that rage and sun's embrace,
We journey on, we find our place.

Old wounds may linger, shadows long,
But with each note, we craft a song.
The compass spins, yet points the truth,
Embracing dreams, we paint our youth.

In valleys deep and mountains high,
We learn to dream, we learn to fly.
In every scar, a story told,
The compass guides us through the bold.

So let us walk with open eyes,
And read the lessons in the skies.
With hope as fuel, we brave the night,
For through experience, we find our light.

Whirls of Memory

In a dance of dust and time,
Whispers echo, soft and prime.
Moments twirl, like leaves in breeze,
In the heart, they never cease.

Faces fade yet never lost,
Each laugh a treasure, every cost.
Snapshots taken, frozen frames,
In the mind, they're still the same.

The scent of rain, the taste of sun,
In every pause, the world's begun.
Whirling soft, the colors blend,
In memory's dance, there is no end.

Journeys taken with the glow,
Of friends we cherish, tales we sow.
Through shadows cast and light adored,
In whirls of memory, hearts are poured.

A tapestry of joy and tears,
Woven tightly through the years.
In every spin, we find our place,
In whirls of memory, we embrace.

The Harmony of Companions

Together we rise, a symphony,
Voices blend in sweet harmony.
In laughter shared, in silence kept,
Through every promise, secrets swept.

Like seasons shift, our bond remains,
In joy and sorrow, love sustains.
Across the miles, through thick and thin,
In every battle, we will win.

Each note we play, a story shines,
Strings entwined, life's grand designs.
With open hearts, we know the face,
Of unity in every space.

The rhythm flows, and time proves kind,
In quiet moments, peace we find.
In the dance of life, we take our stand,
The harmony of companions, hand in hand.

When storms may come and skies turn gray,
We face the dark, we find our way.
In trust and laughter, love expands,
In harmony, our spirit stands.

Ripening Friendship

Like fruit that hangs in warm sunlight,
Friendship grows, a wondrous sight.
With roots entwined beneath the ground,
In laughter and tears, we are bound.

As seasons change and winds will blow,
In every smile, our bond will grow.
Cherished moments, ripe and sweet,
In every heartbeat, we compete.

Through challenges, we find the strength,
Together, we will go the length.
In shadows cast, we find our glow,
Ripening friendship, gently flows.

Like vines that twist, and flowers bloom,
In every breath, love finds its room.
Through trials faced and dreams reaped,
In friendship, our hearts are steeped.

So let us hold this bond so dear,
In every laugh and every tear.
As years unfold, let's celebrate,
Ripening friendship, never too late.

Seasons of Change

Leaves turn gold, as summer fades,
Crisp air whispers, in twilight glades.
Frost kisses blooms with icy breath,
Nature's dance, a cycle of death.

Spring unveils a vibrant bloom,
Life emerges from winter's gloom.
Sunlight sparkles on streams anew,
The earth awakens, fresh and true.

Summer blazes with warmth and light,
Days stretch long, embracing night.
Children laugh, their joy so pure,
In golden fields, their spirits soar.

Autumn brings a harvest feast,
Colors burst, nature's boldest beast.
Pumpkins sit on porches proudly,
While the winds hum, soft and cloudly.

Each season shifts, a gentle hand,
Guiding life across the land.
In every change, a story told,
A tapestry of life unfolds.

The Color of Companionship

In laughter shared, our hearts entwine,
A bond that grows, both yours and mine.
Through stormy nights and sunny days,
Friendship blooms in countless ways.

A gentle touch, a knowing glance,
In every silence, a sweet dance.
Together we face each ebb and flow,
With every moment, our spirits grow.

Colors blend like a painter's hue,
Every shade reflects me and you.
In trials faced, we stand as one,
In the warmth of love, we have won.

When shadows stretch and doubts arise,
Your voice shines bright, a guiding prize.
Hand in hand, we chase the light,
Companionship makes every fight right.

Through all the seasons, here we stand,
In every moment, hand in hand.
The color of love, bold and bright,
A masterpiece painted in pure delight.

Moments Painted in Memory

Fleeting whispers, a soft embrace,
In the quiet, we find our place.
Captured seconds, forever hold,
Stories of love, waiting to be told.

Sunset glows on the horizon wide,
Memories linger, time our guide.
Footprints left on sandy shores,
Echoes of laughter, welcome roars.

A gentle rain on a summer's eve,
In every drop, the heart believes.
Moments shared, both joy and pain,
Pieces of us, like gentle rain.

With every glance, a spark ignites,
Familiar faces, soft, warm lights.
Carved in hearts, through thick and thin,
Timeless treasures where we've been.

Time may fade the vibrant hues,
Yet memories linger, never lose.
In every heartbeat, a soft refrain,
Moments painted, forever remain.

The Symphony of Sincerity

Truth resounds like a vibrant chord,
In every word, our hopes restored.
Notes of kindness, a melody played,
In the quiet moments, sincerity laid.

With open hearts, we share our song,
In the symphony, we all belong.
Harmony blooms in every chance,
As spirits dance in a timeless trance.

Every look speaks volumes clear,
In connection deep, all fear disappears.
Voices rise, in unison strong,
In the realm of truth, we all belong.

A genuine smile, a caring deed,
In every gesture, we plant a seed.
Sincerity shines like the morning dew,
Reflecting warmth in all we do.

Together we weave this grand ballet,
Through every night, into the day.
The symphony plays, soft and bright,
Guided by love, a pure delight.

A Symphony of Souls

In the silence, whispers rise,
Melodies dance under the skies.
Notes of joy intertwine and swell,
In harmony, our spirits dwell.

Voices echo, soft and clear,
Binding hearts that draw near.
Each chord strikes a different tone,
Together, we are never alone.

Fingers brush across the strings,
Creating magic that life brings.
A symphony of dreams takes flight,
Guiding us through the night.

Rhythms pulse in every heart,
Playing roles, each a part.
In this grand and sacred hall,
We find our place and stand tall.

As the curtain starts to fall,
We remember each gentle call.
A symphony that never dies,
In unity, our love will rise.

The Labyrinth of Laughter

In twists and turns, we find our way,
Laughter echoes, come what may.
Through alleys of joy, shadows play,
Every corner holds a new sway.

Bubbles burst with cheery glee,
Moments shared, just you and me.
In this maze of light and sound,
A treasure of joy is always found.

Chasing echoes, we run and whirl,
A tapestry of laughter unfurl.
Each corner hides a playful jest,
In this labyrinth, we are blessed.

With every giggle, worries cease,
In this chaos, we find peace.
Laughter leads us hand in hand,
Together, we forever stand.

As daylight fades into the night,
We carry laughter, our true light.
In the twists of life, we'll roam,
In laughter's arms, we find our home.

Sunshine Through the Gaps

Amidst the clouds, rays break free,
Sunshine shines where hearts can see.
Through every crack, light starts to play,
Chasing the shadows of the day.

With gentle warmth, it fills the air,
Whispering secrets, soft and rare.
Illuminating paths once dark,
Guiding hope like a timeless spark.

In the spaces that life creates,
Sunshine dances; it radiates.
A golden touch upon the skin,
Transforming lives from deep within.

Each moment kissed by light divine,
Creates a space where hearts align.
Through the gaps, we breathe in peace,
Finding solace, sweet release.

So let the sun spill through the panes,
Casting colors that break the chains.
In every gap, let love expand,
In sunshine's glow, together we stand.

Mosaic of Heartbeats

Each heartbeat tells a tale unique,
A rhythm found in every streak.
Colors blend in a vibrant weave,
In this mosaic, we believe.

Fragments of dreams from every soul,
Together they make a perfect whole.
Brushed in shades of laughter and tears,
Creating art that spans the years.

In every pulse, a story flows,
Whispers of joy and pain it shows.
A canvas rich with hues of love,
Guided gently by stars above.

So let us dance to this sweet sound,
In every heartbeat, we are found.
A tapestry that time can't sever,
In this mosaic, we're together.

With every thump, our spirits soar,
Connected deeply at the core.
In this artwork, life unfolds,
A beautiful story forever told.

Notes in a Shared Melody

In the quiet dusk of evening,
Soft whispers dance in twilight's glow.
Harmony binds our hearts together,
A gentle tune that we both know.

Each moment shared, a note is penned,
Filling pages in the air.
Your laughter rings like chimes of joy,
Creating music everywhere.

When shadows loom and doubts arise,
We find strength in the rhythm's flow.
With every beat, our spirits lift,
Creating warmth in winter's snow.

Through life's wild, twisting journey,
Our symphony will ever play.
In every rise and every fall,
Your voice will guide me on my way.

So let us write our timeless song,
With love embedded on each line.
In every note, a memory grows,
A melody forever divine.

Sketches of Affection

With gentle strokes on canvas wide,
I paint with hues of softest light.
Each color tells a story sweet,
Of moments shared, both pure and bright.

A laughing child, a warm embrace,
The sparkle in a lover's eye.
In every sketch, your essence lives,
A masterpiece that never dies.

Through seasons change, the brush still moves,
Capturing time in fleeting grace.
Each line a whisper of our hearts,
Tracing love's journey, every trace.

Though shadows sometimes cross the page,
Your presence shines through every dark.
In art, we find our truth revealed,
Where love ignites its glowing spark.

So let us sketch our dreams anew,
With every stroke, our lives entwined.
In every frame, a sigh of peace,
A work of art, together signed.

The Light of Loyalty

In a world where shadows linger,
Your faith shines bright, a guiding star.
A beacon in the darkest hours,
With you, I know just who we are.

Through storms that rage and winds that howl,
Your strength provides a steady hand.
With every trial we face as one,
Together we will always stand.

In silent vows, our hearts entwined,
A bond that only grows with time.
In laughter shared and tears embraced,
Our loyalty is sweet as rhyme.

Though paths may twist and turn ahead,
I know your heart will stay with mine.
In every chapter that we write,
Our trust will always brightly shine.

So let us walk through life as friends,
Through sunshine bright and fading light.
In loyalty, we find our peace,
Together, we will face the night.

Embers of Understanding

In the silence of the evening,
Soft glows flicker, lives entwined.
The warmth of words, a gentle spark,
Illuminates the hearts that bind.

With every glance, we share a tale,
In quiet moments, truths unfold.
Understanding grows, an ancient fire,
In every story that is told.

Though journeys take us far apart,
The embers glow with timeless grace.
In the warmth of shared compassion,
We find our home, our sacred space.

When clouds may gather overhead,
And doubts may whisper in the night,
Your gaze will anchor me once more,
Rekindling hope, a source of light.

So let us cherish every ember,
Each flicker, bright, a bond anew.
In understanding, love will flourish,
A flame that always guides us through.

The Garden of Trust

In the garden where we stand,
Roots entwined beneath the sand,
Whispers of promises made,
In sunlight and in shade.

Petals bloom with colors bright,
Every worry takes its flight,
Trust, a seed we gently sow,
In the warmth, our hearts will grow.

Through the storms that come our way,
We will stand, come what may,
Facing winds, we hold on tight,
In each other, we find light.

Buds of hope begin to sprout,
With each laugh and every shout,
In this haven, we are free,
Together, just you and me.

So let's plant our dreams with care,
In this garden, love will share,
A bond that time cannot erase,
In trust, we find our place.

Pairs in the Quantum Realm

In the depths of cosmic dance,
Pairs of particles in chance,
Entangled threads, a secret weave,
In mystery, we believe.

With a twist of fate and time,
Every echo, every rhyme,
Silent whispers of the night,
In stardust, our dreams take flight.

Quantum leaps through realms unseen,
Dancing beams of light serene,
In the void, we find a spark,
Through the shadows, we ignite.

Frequencies that pulse and sway,
Guide our hearts along the way,
Pairs united, never bound,
In this magic, we are found.

In the realm where time dissolves,
Mysteries of life evolves,
Hand in hand, we traverse space,
In this dance, we find our grace.

Reflections of Shared Journeys

On the path where footsteps blend,
Journeys start and journeys end,
Moments shared in gentle grace,
In each smile, we find our place.

Through the valleys, up the hills,
Every challenge, every thrill,
Hand in hand, we've walked along,
In our hearts, a shared song.

Mirrors show our laughter bright,
Casting shadows in the light,
Every tear, a story told,
In our bond, love's worth more than gold.

With each twist and turn we roam,
In the world, we've made our home,
Reflections of our souls collide,
In this journey, side by side.

In the echoes of our past,
Every moment, meant to last,
Guided by our hearts' embrace,
In reflections, we find grace.

The Chorus of Understanding

In the silence, voices blend,
Harmony, our hearts extend,
With each note, a truth revealed,
In this choir, love is healed.

From the shadows, we emerge,
In every sigh, a soft surge,
Listening with open hearts,
In this dance, we play our parts.

Threads of trust weave through the night,
Bridging gaps with pure insight,
Melodies of deep connection,
In each chorus, deep affection.

Speak the words we need to say,
In the light of every day,
Through the highs and through the lows,
In understanding, love still grows.

As we rise, our spirits soar,
Together, we can offer more,
A chorus strong, a timeless song,
In this journey, we belong.

The Echo of Shared Laughter

In the air, joy swirls bright,
Moments shared, hearts take flight.
Cascades of giggles dance around,
In this warmth, love is found.

Memories woven, soft and warm,
In the storm, a sheltering charm.
Every chuckle a thread so thin,
Binding souls, where joy begins.

Beneath the stars, our laughter sings,
Bonded tightly, the joy it brings.
Fleeting echoes, sweet and clear,
In these moments, we hold dear.

Together we stumble, we stand tall,
In the chorus of laughter, we answer the call.
With every note, the world fades away,
In the echo, forever we stay.

Through every laugh, our spirits soar,
With every joy, we seek for more.
In the tapestry of life we weave,
The echo remains, we believe.

Windows to Each Other's Souls

In your gaze, worlds unfold,
Stories whisper, secrets told.
Windows open, hearts align,
In this silence, love does shine.

Every glance, a gentle grace,
Reflecting dreams we dare to chase.
In stillness, we find our way,
Through your eyes, light of day.

The depths we share, profound and true,
Each look exchanged, a vivid hue.
In this space, we bare our fears,
In the silence, hear our tears.

Together we're lost, yet we're found,
In the silence, a sacred sound.
Through the glass, we see what's real,
In each moment, love's appeal.

In the twilight, our spirits dance,
Captured in this timeless glance.
Windows open, let love flow,
In each other's souls, we grow.

Tides of Togetherness

With each wave, we rise and fall,
Surfing dreams, answering the call.
Tides of love, strong and free,
In this ocean, you and me.

Soft whispers of the sea breeze,
Guiding hearts with graceful ease.
With every tide, we find our way,
Together, come what may.

In the currents, we twine and turn,
Lessons of love, forever we learn.
Each ebb and flow, a dance so fine,
In the rhythm, our hearts entwine.

On the shore, hand in hand,
Braving storms, we make our stand.
With every surge, our bonds grow tight,
In the waters, pure delight.

Together we anchor, strong and true,
In this journey, just me and you.
Tides of togetherness, forever to share,
In the vastness, we boldly dare.

Threads of Connection

In the fabric of life, we weave,
Woven threads that never leave.
Stitch by stitch, our tales unfold,
In every hue, stories told.

Like silken strands, so interlaced,
Colors bright, with love embraced.
Tangled paths that lead us near,
In this weave, we hold dear.

Over mountains, through the streams,
In each moment, shared dreams gleam.
Threads of laughter, joy and pain,
In the tapestry, life's refrain.

Each connection, a vibrant thread,
Binding souls, where love is bred.
In the loom of time, we find our place,
Through every stitch, an endless grace.

Together we weave, together we mend,
In every fray, we find a friend.
Threads of connection, strong and wide,
In this fabric, love will abide.

The Balance of Give and Take

In the dance of life we share,
A gentle push, a tender care.
What we take and what we give,
In harmony, together we live.

Moments exchanged like cherished coins,
In laughter's echo, friendship joins.
With open hearts, we find our way,
Counting blessings day by day.

Sometimes the scales may tip or sway,
Yet in the heart, love finds its way.
To balance joy with grief so deep,
In every secret, promises keep.

Through storms that test our fragile bond,
A silent vow, our spirits respond.
In every tear, in every ache,
We forge the strength of give and take.

So here we stand, steadfast and true,
In pulses shared, we both renew.
For life's a tapestry, brightly sewn,
In each thread, together we've grown.

Ribbons of Remembrance

Tied with care, memories gleam,
Ribbons of light in daylight's beam.
Whispers of laughter, stories unfold,
In every memory, love is bold.

Colors of time wrapped around,
Moments captured, blissfully found.
Each ribbon tells a tale anew,
In every hue, we find the true.

With delicate hands, we tie the knot,
Binding our souls in every thought.
Through seasons passed, we hold them dear,
In ribbons of joy, laughter, and tear.

As shadows dance and dreams take flight,
We gather memories, day and night.
With every twist, a parting glance,
In ribbons of love, we find our chance.

So let us weave, as daylight fades,
In ribbons bright, where friendship parades.
For every thread a life embraced,
In care and joy, we are interlaced.

Diagrams of Trust

In quiet lines, our hearts align,
Sketching dreams, so pure, divine.
With every dot, a bond is made,
In diagrams, our fears allayed.

A pencil marks with gentle grace,
The trials faced, a sacred space.
Within the shapes, a story sings,
In designs of trust, hope takes wings.

Connections drawn with every breath,
In honest lines, we conquer death.
Through curves and angles, we persist,
In every outline, love exists.

So let us share, through ink and time,
Our fragile hearts, a steady climb.
In diagrams where we belong,
Together we rise, forever strong.

In trust we find our paths entwined,
With every sketch, our fates aligned.
Through paper trails and inked delight,
Our diagrams glow in endless light.

The Wind Beneath Our Wings

In gentle whispers, breezes soar,
Lifting spirits, forevermore.
With every gust, we take to flight,
In unity, we spark the light.

Together we dance on clouds above,
Fueled by courage, strength, and love.
As feathers brush against the sky,
On wings of hope, we learn to fly.

In storms that rage and skies that dark,
We find the routes, we leave our mark.
Through trials faced, our hearts will sing,
Embracing all that life will bring.

With every shared dream, we ascend,
The bond unbroken, on it depends.
For each heartbeat fuels the flight,
Together we rise, hearts burning bright.

So feel the wind, let it embrace,
In every journey, find your place.
For in the skies, our spirits cling,
To be the wind beneath our wings.

Bridges of Understanding

In silence, we build our ways,
Across the chasms of our days.
With patience, we mend the seams,
Holding tight to shared dreams.

In shadows of doubt, we stand,
Reaching out, a helping hand.
Voices soft, yet strong they sing,
The warmth that our trust can bring.

Through storms that test our will,
We find strength, our hearts to fill.
With every step upon this ground,
A bond unbroken can be found.

In the echoes of our laughter,
We discover what comes after.
A future bright, a path so clear,
Bridges built with love sincere.

Together, we rise above,
In the light of shared love.
With every whisper, every song,
In unity, we all belong.

In the Wake of Laughter

Laughter dances through the air,
Like sunlight, bright and warm, it's rare.
In moments shared, we find our way,
Each chuckle brightening the day.

A symphony of joy we create,
In every joke, we celebrate.
With faces aglow from pure delight,
We chase away shadows of night.

The echoes linger, sweet and pure,
In every heart, a joyous cure.
In the wake of laughter shared,
Our burdens lighten, souls are bared.

We find connection in each grin,
The warmth of kindness held within.
In giggles soft, our spirits soar,
Reminding us of what's in store.

With each shared moment, we ignite,
A spark of joy, a shared delight.
In the rhythm of our laughter's song,
Together is where we all belong.

The Map of Kindred Souls

In the valleys of the heart,
We chart paths that never part.
With every glance, we navigate,
A bond that time can never break.

Through whispers soft, we find our place,
In each other's warm embrace.
The compass guides us, love's true north,
In kinship's light, we venture forth.

Connections bloom like flowers bright,
In the garden of shared light.
With every step, we tread as one,
In harmony, our journey's begun.

Though storms may rise and winds may blow,
Together, we will always grow.
On this map, our souls entwined,
In every heart, a treasure signed.

With every heartbeat, we align,
In shared moments, pure and fine.
Kindred spirits, hand in hand,
Together, we shall always stand.

Alignments of Hearts

Under the stars, we align,
In the quiet, a love, divine.
With every heartbeat, pulse and flow,
In a rhythm that we both know.

Like constellations in the night,
Our dreams connect, a guiding light.
In the dance of fate, we sway,
Drawing closer day by day.

With gentle truths, we intertwine,
Two souls as one, a sacred sign.
In whispers shared, our thoughts take flight,
Igniting passions, pure delight.

Through challenges, we find our way,
Building strength from what we say.
In the warmth of our shared art,
We find grace in each other's heart.

As day turns night, and dawn breaks bright,
Our love grows deeper, taking flight.
In alignments true, we'll always see,
The beauty in you and me.

Conversations Over Coffee

Steam rises softly, a fragrant embrace,
Words tumble freely, a warm, gentle pace.
Laughter dances lightly, under soft lights,
In shared silences, our hearts take flight.

Mugs clink together, stories unfold,
Each sip a memory, treasured and bold.
Dreams spill like cream, rich and profound,
In our little café, love knows no bound.

Morning glows brighter with each passing word,
In quiet corners, our hopes are stirred.
A tapestry woven with threads of our souls,
In conversations over coffee, we find our roles.

Time slips away, lost in the brew,
The world fades softly, just us two.
Moments grow linger, as shadows play,
In this cherished refuge, I wish to stay.

With every heartbeat, the bond grows strong,
Each shared glance feels like a song.
In the warmth of coffee, we come alive,
In every sip, our spirits thrive.

Storms Before Sunsets

Clouds gather fiercely, a tempest unfolds,
Raindrops like whispers, secrets retold.
Thunder rumbles deeply, a lover's sigh,
In storms before sunsets, we learn to fly.

Darkness envelops, yet hope remains bright,
Colors clash wildly, a dance of the night.
Lightning paints shadows, fierce and alive,
With every struggle, the heart will survive.

The sky starts to clear, soft hues intertwine,
Majestic transitions, nature's design.
In the stillness that follows, peace takes its place,
The beauty of chaos reveals its grace.

Sunlight breaks gently, a golden embrace,
Emerging from worries, we find our space.
In storms before sunsets, life's lessons endure,
For every dark moment, there's always a cure.

Together we stand, through turmoil and calm,
Holding each other, a soothing balm.
In the dance of the elements, we find our song,
In storms before sunsets, we both belong.

The Harmony of Disparate Notes

In a world of chaos, melodies collide,
Each different sound, a unique guiding tide.
Voices blend softly, a symphony whole,
The harmony whispers, touching the soul.

Frequencies flutter, like leaves in the breeze,
Navigating life's rhythms, they aim to please.
Each note is a story, of joy and of pain,
Together they flourish, like sun after rain.

The clamor of life, a beautiful mess,
Yet in the discord, we learn to express.
In moments of quiet, the heart finds its way,
The harmony beckons, come join and play.

From strings to brass, every hue has its sound,
A tapestry woven, where love can be found.
In the dance of the chorus, we learn to unite,
Finding our rhythm, we step into light.

So let every note ring, both bitter and sweet,
In this grand orchestra, our hearts will meet.
The harmony sings of the paths we have tread,
In the tapestry woven, our spirits are fed.

In the Garden of Affection

Flowers bloom brightly, colors so pure,
In this fragrant garden, our hearts feel secure.
Petals unfold gently, love's tender art,
In the garden of affection, we nurture the heart.

Sunlight filters softly, casting warm rays,
Each moment a treasure, in delicate play.
The earth beneath whispers, secrets untold,
In this sacred place, our dreams unfold.

Butterflies flutter, as laughter prevails,
Dancing on breezes, weaving sweet trails.
In stillness we linger, time ceases to flow,
In the garden of affection, our spirits will grow.

Seasons may shift, as moments do pass,
Yet the roots of our love, will forever last.
Through sun and through rain, we cultivate trust,
In the garden of affection, this bond is a must.

With each gentle touch, our hearts intertwine,
In this blooming paradise, your hand is in mine.
Together we flourish, through joy and through strife,
In the garden of affection, we blossom in life.

What We Share in Silence

In quiet moments, hearts align,
Words unspoken, yet divine.
A gentle touch, a knowing glance,
In stillness, we find our dance.

Beneath the stars, we gaze above,
A bond that's crafted, built on love.
The world outside fades away,
In silence, we choose to stay.

With every breath, a tale unfolds,
In shared silence, warmth enfolds.
A whisper soft, a secret shared,
In our silence, we are paired.

Though words may fail, our spirits blend,
In quietude, we apprehend.
The spaces in between convey,
In silence's grip, we find our way.

Together here, where stillness reigns,
In silent realms, love breaks the chains.
What we share, a sacred trust,
In silence, we rise, as we must.

Weaving Dreams in Twilight

As daylight wanes, we dream awake,
In twilight's glow, new worlds we make.
Stars peep through the fading light,
Our hopes take wing, bold and bright.

With every thread, our visions blend,
In twilight's arms, we transcend.
Whispers of fate, weaving through night,
Our dreams unfold, taking flight.

Colors swirl in dusky skies,
In twilight's warmth, our spirits rise.
We sketch our dreams, both bold and free,
In this sacred realm, you and me.

The fabric of time, we intertwine,
As shadows play, our hearts align.
With each soft breath, our wishes soar,
In twilight's dance, we explore.

Together we weave, a tapestry grand,
In fading light, we make our stand.
For dreams ignited in dusky hues,
In twilight's embrace, we choose.

The Tides of Together

With every wave, our spirits flow,
In currents strong, together we go.
The ocean's song, a timeless bind,
In tides of love, our hearts entwined.

As sand shifts beneath our feet,
Each moment shared, a heartbeat sweet.
In every rise, and gentle fall,
The tides of us will always call.

Together we'll brave the stormy seas,
With laughter and love, tranquil breeze.
For in the depths, we find our truth,
In each embrace, eternal youth.

Though storms may come to toss and turn,
In every wave, our fires burn.
For hand in hand, we face the fight,
In tides of together, we find our light.

And as the sun dips low and red,
In ocean's arms, we go ahead.
Forever bound, like stars that shine,
In tides of us, our souls align.

Letters Unsent

In the quiet, words take flight,
Letters penned in soft moonlight.
Unsent messages, hearts laid bare,
In ink and dreams, I find you there.

Each line a whisper, secrets kept,
In silent echoes, tears are wept.
Pages crumpled, dreams on hold,
Unwritten tales of love retold.

The ink may fade, but feelings stay,
In letters unsent, they whisper, sway.
For every word I dared not send,
In thoughts, our hearts forever blend.

Beneath the stars, my heart reveals,
The truth of love that time conceals.
Though letters wait, my love is real,
In silent thoughts, it's you I feel.

With every sunset, I release,
These unsent letters finding peace.
In dreams, you read what's in my heart,
In every pause, we're not apart.

Bonds Unbroken

Through storms we weather, side by side,
In strength and love, our hearts abide.
With every trial, our spirits rise,
In bonds unbroken, love defies.

The years may pass like fleeting days,
But in your eyes, my heart always stays.
Each memory crafted, a sacred thread,
In bonds unbroken, love is fed.

Moments shared, both joy and pain,
Through laughter bright and warmest rain.
In silence deep, or songs we sing,
In bonds unbroken, hope takes wing.

As seasons shift and time moves on,
Our connection holds, forever strong.
In every heartbeat, a promise made,
In bonds unbroken, never to fade.

With every breath, I choose to stay,
In your embrace, come what may.
Together we stand, for all we've spoken,
In love's embrace, our bonds unbroken.

Mosaics of Memories

Fragments of laughter, scattered bright,
Echoes of whispers in the soft night.
Faded photographs tell tales untold,
A tapestry woven with love and gold.

Each piece a treasure, carefully kept,
Moments we cherish, the tears we wept.
Colors entwined, a beautiful blend,
In this mosaic, we never end.

Through memories' lens, we find our way,
In shadows and light, we choose to stay.
We stitch our stories with each heartbeat,
A dance of the past, forever sweet.

Time may erode, but we stand firm,
In each memory, a glowing germ.
Building a future from remnants of yore,
Mosaics of life, forever we explore.

Lanterns in the Dark

Flickering flames, casting soft glow,
Guiding our steps through the depths below.
In silence we wander, hand in hand,
Lanterns of hope in a shadowed land.

Each flicker beckons, a spark of trust,
Illuminating paths when dreams are dust.
We share our fears with whispered prayers,
With lanterns aloft, we banish despair.

As stars above fade, our lights stay bright,
Through storms and shadows, we find the light.
Together we shine, a radiant pair,
In the darkest corners, love's always there.

Guided by lanterns, our spirits soar,
Brighter with courage, we seek for more.
In the tapestry woven, each thread we mark,
Together we linger, lanterns in the dark.

The Puzzle of Us

Pieces lay scattered, around on the floor,
Edges of laughter and memories galore.
Each curve a secret, each corner a tale,
The puzzle of us, our hearts will prevail.

In hues of affection, we fit just right,
Assembling fragments, igniting the night.
With patience we search, through layers so deep,
Finding connection, the promises we keep.

Every misfit moment brings laughter anew,
We learn from the struggles, from joy and from blue.
With every completed section, we grow,
The puzzle of us brings warmth to the flow.

Together we conquer, the pieces align,
Building a love that is tender, divine.
In the gallery of hearts, our masterpiece stands,
The puzzle of us, always hand in hand.

Waves of Warmth

Gentle caresses, the sun on our skin,
Waves of warmth wash over, a soothing din.
In oceans of laughter, we drift and we sway,
Embracing the moments that carry the day.

The tide pulls us close, a dance so sublime,
In rhythm we move, as if frozen in time.
With each crashing wave, our spirits ignite,
In the heart of the storm, we find our light.

Salt in the breeze, a kiss from the sea,
Waves of warmth whisper, "Always be free."
Together we wander, through treasure and pain,
In the tide's sweet embrace, our love will remain.

Through ebbs and flows, we cling to the shore,
Each wave brings us closer, forever it soars.
In the ocean of life, we're never apart,
Waves of warmth cradle the depths of our heart.

Reflections in a Shared Mirror

In quiet depths, we gaze and see,
The echoes of our history.
Two souls entwined, a single view,
In mirrored light, we blend and brew.

Moments caught in silver sheen,
Shadows dance where we've both been.
Secrets shared beyond the veil,
In every triumph, every tale.

Frames of joy, both large and small,
Reflected dreams in shadows fall.
With every glance, understanding grows,
In this shared mirror, love bestows.

Laughter rings, a vibrant sound,
In every smile, our truth is found.
We stand as one, in life's embrace,
In this reflection, we find grace.

Threads of fate in silver spun,
Two hearts beating, forever one.
In each ripple, our stories blend,
In this mirror, we transcend.

The Dance of Kindred Spirits

With every twirl, our souls ignite,
In rhythm's pulse, we find the light.
Hands entwined, we lose our fears,
In every step, the joy appears.

Around the floor, the world dissolves,
In this moment, our love evolves.
Whispers shared in silent grace,
In every glance, we find our place.

The music swells, it calls us near,
In every note, I feel you here.
In laughter's dance, we weave our tale,
With every spin, we shall not fail.

Time stands still as we collide,
In this whirl, we choose to glide.
No maps or plans, just hearts in tune,
As kindred spirits, we are immune.

Let the world fade, let worries cease,
In this dance, we find our peace.
Together we sway, beneath the stars,
In this union, we heal our scars.

Moments that Paint Our Bond

In brushstrokes bold, colors cascade,
Moments shared, like memories made.
With every hue, our laughter sings,
In vibrant shades, our story clings.

Each canvas holds a sacred space,
Where time stands still, in love's embrace.
A palette rich with joy and pain,
In every stroke, we find our gain.

This masterpiece, it's ours alone,
Through trials faced, our spirits grown.
In every line, a tale defined,
Moments crafted, hand in hand aligned.

With brighter strokes, we chase the light,
In shadows deep, we find our fight.
Each layer thickens, tells our truth,
In artful expressions, we find our youth.

As time will fade the colors bright,
Our bond remains, a guiding light.
In every moment, a brush of fate,
Together, we'll create, never wait.

Unfolding Pages of Trust

In whispered words, our stories unfold,
Each page turned with trust untold.
With ink of hope, we write our dreams,
In every chapter, love redeems.

Together we pen each silent plea,
In this book, just you and me.
Time's gentle hand guides our quill,
In every line, our hearts fulfill.

Through storms we've crossed, we find our tale,
In every trial, we never fail.
Bound by love, our pages blend,
In this story, there's no end.

With trust as ink and faith as thread,
We build a world where dreams are fed.
Each moment lived, a timeless rhyme,
In these pages, we conquer time.

With every word, we come alive,
In this trust, we always thrive.
Unfolding tales, forever ours,
In this narrative, we reach the stars.

The Fabric of Fellowship

In threads of laughter, we entwine,
A bond of hearts, both yours and mine.
Through trials faced, we stand as one,
Together we rise, our journey begun.

Wrapped in trust, each story shared,
In gentle whispers, love declared.
Through storms we bravely navigate,
United we stand, we celebrate.

In moments small, our joy is found,
In every hug, our strength is bound.
With hands held tight, we face the night,
In fellowship true, we find the light.

As seasons change, our roots run deep,
In shared memories, our spirits leap.
A tapestry rich, woven of dreams,
In the fabric of life, our love redeems.

So let us cherish this sacred thread,
With every word that's kindly said.
In fellowship's grace, we truly thrive,
Together we flourish, forever alive.

Silhouettes of Support

In shadows cast by guiding light,
We find our strength in shared insight.
Through whispered fears and evening talks,
Together we walk, our hearts unlocks.

With every step, in silence, bold,
Our stories of warmth and courage told.
In laughter's echo, we stand tall,
In silhouettes soft, we'll never fall.

A hand to hold when spirits wane,
In every loss, we share the pain.
Through joy and sorrow, side by side,
In unity true, our hearts abide.

In trials faced, we find our way,
Through storms endured, come what may.
In the tapestry of life, we grow,
In silhouettes bright, our spirits flow.

So let us cherish this sacred bond,
In every whisper, love responds.
In the shadows, we create a glow,
In silhouettes of support, we grow.

Vows Under the Moon

Beneath the stars, our promises bloom,
In soft twilight, we banish gloom.
With whispered vows, our hearts entwine,
Under the moon, your hand in mine.

Through silver beams, our love ignites,
In sacred moments, our souls take flight.
With every glance, a spark is born,
In this embrace, our fears are torn.

As shadows dance, we pledge our truth,
In every heartbeat, we embrace youth.
Together we dream, with hope anew,
Vows under the moon, just me and you.

With every sigh, we trace our fate,
In radiant moonlight, we celebrate.
So here we stand, hearts open wide,
In love's pure light, forever guide.

So let us cherish this sacred night,
In vows embraced, our future bright.
Under the moon, our souls align,
In love's sweet promise, forever shine.

The Tapestry We Weave

In colors bright, our lives entwine,
A tapestry rich, both yours and mine.
With every thread, a story holds,
In love's warm embrace, our future unfolds.

With gentle hands, we shape our fate,
In every moment, we celebrate.
Across the fabric, our dreams align,
In the tapestry woven, love's design.

Through laughter and tears, we stitch our days,
In vibrant hues, our hearts ablaze.
With every pattern, a tale to share,
In the tapestry of life, we care.

As seasons change, and time moves on,
In every sunrise, a new dawn.
Together we stand, in harmony,
In the tapestry woven, love sets free.

So let us cherish each thread we spin,
In every moment, let love begin.
Through the fabric of life, we shall weave,
In this grand design, we dare believe.

The Language of Unseen Threads

In whispers soft, we weave our fate,
Silent bonds that intertwine and create.
Echoes dance through the air we share,
Invisible cords, a tender affair.

With every glance, a story unfolds,
In the gentle pull, our truth is told.
Unseen threads, they guide our way,
In the quiet spaces where hearts play.

A tapestry rich in colors bright,
Woven with care, in day and night.
Through trials faced, we stand aligned,
In the loom of time, our souls entwined.

Each moment holds a sacred thread,
In laughter shared and tears we've shed.
The language spoken, without a sound,
In the heart's echo, we are found.

Unseen threads bind our lives anew,
In the fabric of dreams, they guide us through.
With faith and love, we journey far,
Together woven, forever a star.

Kindness in the Kaleidoscope

A shift of light, a gentle hue,
In every heart, kindness breaks through.
Fractals of laughter, colors unite,
Painting the world in warmth and light.

In moments shared, we find our way,
In tiny gestures, love does sway.
Through prisms of hope, we see the best,
Kindness blooms, a heartfelt quest.

Reflections bright, with smiles that shine,
In the kaleidoscope, our souls entwine.
Every small act, a powerful spark,
Illuminating paths, igniting the dark.

We gather strength from sun and rain,
In cycles of joy, in cycles of pain.
A mosaic of hearts, diverse yet whole,
In kindness's embrace, we reclaim our soul.

So let us dance in colors bold,
In the warmth of kindness, we break the mold.
In every heartbeat, let love unfold,
A legacy of care, far richer than gold.

Horizon of Our Connection

Upon the hill, the dawn does break,
A canvas wide, for hearts awake.
With every sunrise, new hopes arise,
In the horizon where our dream lies.

We touch the sky, with fingers outstretched,
In shared whispers, our spirits are fetched.
A bridge of souls, where moments dwell,
In each heartbeat, there's magic to tell.

Through valleys deep and mountains wide,
In rhythm and pulse, we walk side by side.
The horizon near, yet forever far,
Together we chase the guiding star.

In twilight's glow, our shadows merge,
A testament of love, a gentle surge.
With every step, we rewrite fate,
In the horizon, we patiently wait.

For as the sun sets, our story's spun,
In the tapestry woven, we are one.
In the horizon's embrace, love is found,
In connection deep, we are unbound.

Tides of Trust and Time

The ocean's dance, a steady tide,
In trust we sail, with dreams as guide.
Each wave that crashes, echoes our song,
With the pull of the moon, where we belong.

Hours drift like sand through open hands,
In moments seized, our truth withstands.
Each whisper shared, like shells on the shore,
In the haven of trust, we seek for more.

As tides roll in, they teach us to bend,
In the cycle of time, we learn to mend.
With each ebb and flow, knowledge accrues,
In trust's gentle arms, we cannot lose.

The horizon calls, a promise so bright,
In the depth of the sea, we find our light.
With every heartbeat, the currents align,
In the tides of trust, our spirits entwine.

Let us navigate through storms and bliss,
In the ocean of time, find strength in the kiss.
For together we sail, hearts open wide,
In the waves of trust, forever we ride.

The Mosaic of Togetherness

In colors bright, we find our way,
Pieces fit, like night and day.
Hands held tight, we walk as one,
A tapestry, our hearts have spun.

Through trials faced, we stand so strong,
In unity, we all belong.
With every step, our spirits rise,
We weave the threads that unify.

Laughter echoes, joy we share,
In moments real, we show we care.
Through ups and downs, we find our grace,
Together, we create our space.

Let dreams ignite, like stars that gleam,
In harmony, we chase our dream.
With love as glue, our bond won't break,
A fortress built, for our hearts' sake.

In gentle whispers, hearts will blend,
In every loss, we find our mend.
This mosaic shines, both bright and true,
In every hue, I find you too.

The Sky of Shared Dreams

Beneath the vast, a canvas wide,
We paint our hopes, with dreams that glide.
As stars collide, a dance unfolds,
In every night, our story's told.

We soar as one, on wings of light,
Through stormy days and peaceful nights.
Above the clouds, our visions soar,
In endless love, we seek for more.

The winds may change, but still we strive,
In shared ambitions, we feel alive.
With every dawn, new colors bloom,
In this great sky, there's always room.

With every heartbeat, dreams align,
Together, we are so divine.
The universe whispers in our ears,
In every laughter, wash away fears.

So let us fly, hand in hand,
Across this sky, we make our stand.
In hope's embrace, our spirits gleam,
Together, we'll chase that shared dream.

Traces of Kindness

In gentle words, a touch so light,
We leave behind kindness in flight.
A smile exchanged, a hand to lend,
In every act, our hearts we send.

Through silent gestures, small and sweet,
Kind deeds arise in strangers we meet.
The world transforms in softer hues,
With every kindness, love renews.

In darkest hours, a brightened glow,
A simple act can help us grow.
From heart to heart, the ripples spread,
In every kind word, hope is fed.

So take a chance to share your light,
In every shadow, make it bright.
For traces left may change a fate,
In kindness found, we resonate.

With every footprint, paths we've crossed,
In love's embrace, we find what's lost.
Together we sing, this sweet refrain,
In traces of kindness, we gain.

The Echo of Laughter

In joyous sounds, our spirits play,
The echo of laughter lights the way.
From silly jokes to stories spun,
In shared delight, we come undone.

With every giggle, hearts take flight,
In rooms aglow with pure delight.
The simple joys, they bind us tight,
In laughter's grip, we find our light.

In moments shared, the world stands still,
In echoes clear, time bends to will.
Through ups and downs, we rise above,
In every chuckle, we find love.

So let us cherish these joyful sounds,
In laughter's warmth, true peace abounds.
For every smile is like a song,
In echoes of laughter, we belong.

In every heart, that joy resides,
In endless waves, the laughter hides.
Together we dance, we sing, we cheer,
In the echo of laughter, we persevere.

Ripples of Resonance

In quiet streams, the echoes play,
A gentle breeze, a soft ballet.
Each drop reflects the sun's warm glow,
Creating art in ebb and flow.

Whispers dance on water's face,
Memories weave in time and space.
A harmony that calls to me,
In every wave, a symphony.

The heart knows how to resonate,
With every sound, a vital state.
We share our laughter, tears, and sighs,
In ripples formed beneath the skies.

An ocean deep, emotions swell,
In every calm, there's a story to tell.
The tides of love and friendship meet,
In every pulse, in every beat.

Listen close to nature's song,
Where every note feels like it belongs.
In the quiet, find your peace,
And let the ripples never cease.

The Lighthouse of Support

In stormy seas, a beacon shines,
A guiding light where hope aligns.
Through darkest nights, it stands so tall,
Reminding us we'll never fall.

The waves may crash, the winds may roar,
But here we find a steady shore.
With arms outstretched and hearts so wide,
Together, we can turn the tide.

A flicker bright, a warmth to share,
In times of doubt, we're standing there.
The lighthouse calls, "You're not alone,"
In every heart, a safe haven's known.

With every storm, we rise anew,
In the struggle, our strength shines through.
Together we will always stand,
As anchors firm, hand in hand.

Through fog and fear, our spirits soar,
With love and trust, we'll find the shore.
The lighthouse stays, a symbol bright,
Of steadfast love, a guiding light.

Pathways of Emotion

Through winding trails, our feelings flow,
We navigate where hearts can grow.
Each step we take, a story told,
In whispers soft and glances bold.

Through laughter's song and sorrow's ache,
We tread the path that we must make.
In every bend, a lesson learned,
In every turn, a fire burned.

Our hearts like rivers, course and twist,
In moments shared, we can't resist.
Together, through each high and low,
In depth of feeling, love will show.

We find our way through joy and fear,
With every choice, we bring us near.
In every tear, a seed is sown,
In every smile, we find our home.

The paths we take connect us all,
In rising sun or twilight's call.
Together we explore the ride,
Through pathways of emotion, side by side.

Seeds of Growth

In gentle soil, we plant our dreams,
With tender hope, our spirit beams.
Each seed a whisper of what could be,
In every heart, a chance to see.

The sun will shine, the rain will fall,
In nature's way, we heed the call.
With patience deep, we watch and wait,
As roots entwine, we cultivate.

Through seasons change, we learn to stand,
With every storm, we grow more grand.
In shifting winds, our branches sway,
Reaching for light, come what may.

A garden lush, our visions bloom,
With every color, banishing gloom.
We nurture love in every row,
In seeds of growth, our spirits glow.

Together we thrive, a vibrant place,
In every heartbeat, we find grace.
Through all we face, let's boldly grow,
In unity, our hearts will show.

The Quilt of Shared Moments

In threads of laughter stitched with care,
We weave our dreams into the air.
Each patch a story, vibrant, bright,
A tapestry of joy and light.

The colors blend as days unfold,
In every fold, new tales are told.
With every hug, each gentle touch,
Our quilt of love means so much.

Through storms we stitched, through sunlit days,
In every moment, love displays.
Our fabric strong, it won't unbind,
A testament to hearts entwined.

With every tear, we patch anew,
In shared moments, we find our hue.
Together sewn, forever tight,
A quilt of memories, pure delight.

So here we sit, in cozy warmth,
In our quilt's embrace, we find our charm.
Through time and space, our hearts will stay,
In this quilt, forever play.

Shadows Dancing in the Light

In twilight's glow, shadows softly sway,
They dance to whispers of the day.
Each silhouette tells a tale untold,
In hues of silver, brown, and gold.

The breeze brings secrets from afar,
As day departs, we watch the stars.
Our laughter mingles with the night,
In shadows dancing, hearts take flight.

The rhythm flows, a gentle sign,
As moments blend, you are mine.
Underneath the starlit skies,
In shadows deep, our spirits rise.

With every twirl, the night ignites,
A symphony of soft delights.
In warmth of love, we find our grace,
In shadows dancing, we embrace.

So let the night be our delight,
With every shadow in the light.
Together whole, with hearts so bright,
In shadows dancing, love takes flight.

Stars Aligned Before Us

In velvet skies the stars align,
A cosmic dance, a grand design.
Each twinkle whispers, bold and true,
Destined paths lead me to you.

The universe, with gentle sway,
Unveils its magic every day.
With every breath, we feel the pull,
In starlit dreams, our hearts are full.

As constellations light our way,
We find the strength in love's display.
With every glance, a spark ignites,
In endless night, our future writes.

Through moonlit nights and sunlit days,
The stars above guide us always.
In every heartbeat, every sigh,
In love's embrace, we soar the sky.

So let us dance under this dome,
With stars aligned, we'll find our home.
In the vastness, we are just one,
Together shining, two become one.

Unwritten Chapters of Us

In pages blank, our stories lie,
With every glance, we learn to fly.
An unwritten chapter waits to bloom,
In the spaces 'tween joy and gloom.

The ink is fresh, awaiting fate,
Each moment shared, we celebrate.
With every word, our bond grows tight,
In unwritten chapters, dreams take flight.

The pen in hand, we script our dreams,
In laughter's echo, love redeems.
Our hearts are open, trust our guide,
In unwritten chapters, side by side.

Through stormy nights and sunny beams,
We'll pen our tale with hopeful dreams.
Together on this journey vast,
In unwritten chapters, love will last.

So let us write, where hearts are free,
In every line, you and me.
With every turn of page anew,
Unwritten chapters lead us through.

Footprints in the Sand of Time

Footprints linger on the shore,
Whispers carried by the tide.
In each grain, a memory,
Of journeys where we strive.

Sunset paints the sky with gold,
Moments captured in its glow.
Though the waves may wash away,
The essence still will flow.

Time will fade the marks we leave,
Yet they mold who we become.
Every step a thread we weave,
In life's intricate drum.

The tides may shift, the winds may change,
But our footprints tell a tale.
Of laughter, love, and dreams exchanged,
A melody in the pale.

As we walk this endless path,
Let us cherish every stride.
For in each print, a legacy,
In the sand, forever tied.

The Colors of Our Alleys

In alleys filled with tales untold,
Vibrant hues and shadows dance.
Graffiti whispers stories bold,
With every stroke, a chance.

Brick and mortar hold the past,
With secrets etched in every wall.
A canvas where the hearts are cast,
In silence, they rise and fall.

The scent of spices fills the air,
Cafés hum with life and sound.
In every corner, love and care,
In every crevice, dreams are found.

Children play 'neath skies of blue,
Laughter echoes, bright and clear.
Faces tell a tale anew,
Uniting all who gather near.

As evening falls, the lights ignite,
Transforming alleys into gold.
A vibrant world in fading light,
Where life's rich layers unfold.

Voices of the Unseen

In shadows where the silence breathes,
Whispers float like fragile dreams.
The unseen cry for our hearts' ease,
In gentle, haunting streams.

They tell of love that once was whole,
Of journeys lost, yet still they speak.
In every crack, the stories toll,
For those who feel too weak.

Listen closely to the night,
For echoes linger everywhere.
Each sigh and tear, each fleeting light,
Carrying weight we often bear.

For in the quiet, voices rise,
A chorus woven through the air.
Their songs embrace the bitter skies,
Revealing truths we often spare.

Let's honor those who fade from view,
Their spirits guide us day by day.
For in their stories, judgments brew,
A light that shows the way.

In the Garden of Souls

In a garden where soft breezes sigh,
Each petal speaks, each leaf knows.
Whispers of time beneath the sky,
In serenity, life grows.

Sunlight dances on the dew,
Colorful blooms in gentle grace.
The heart finds peace in every hue,
In this tranquil, sacred space.

Roots reach deep into the earth,
Binding stories of the past.
Each flower tells of love and birth,
In this embrace, we are cast.

The fragrance weaves a tale of hope,
Every breeze a soft caress.
In this sanctuary, we can cope,
Finding solace in nature's dress.

As we wander through this bloom,
Let the garden hold our dreams.
In its arms, we find the room,
Where every soul forever gleams.

Beneath the Canopy of Companionship

In the shade where shadows play,
Laughter dances through the day.
Friendship blooms in gentle hues,
Under skies of vibrant blues.

Whispers shared like rustling leaves,
In this space, our hearts believe.
Together we weather storms and sun,
A bond unbroken, always fun.

Time stands still as moments weave,
In this haven, we believe.
Hands entwined, we face the night,
Guided by our shared light.

The world outside can fade away,
But here, together, we shall stay.
Beneath the canopy so wide,
A sanctuary where souls confide.

With every tale and secret shared,
A roots of trust is gently spared.
In this garden of pure delight,
We grow stronger, day and night.

A Tapestry of Memories

Threads of laughter, woven tight,
Colors vibrant, pure delight.
Each stitch holds a precious tale,
A tapestry where dreams set sail.

Time unfolds in patterns grand,
Moments cherished, hand in hand.
Memories painted across the sky,
In every twist, a sweet goodbye.

The fabric softens as we grow,
Layered stories, ebb and flow.
With each heartbeat, new tales start,
Woven deep within the heart.

Faded threads, yet strong and bold,
A tapestry of love retold.
Fingers trace each flow and fold,
As life's treasures slowly unfold.

In this artwork, life weaves on,
From dusk till the early dawn.
Together we make our mark,
In every seam, a living spark.

The Rhythm of Kindness

In the silence where hearts beat,
Kindness flows, a steady beat.
Gentle gestures, soft and pure,
In this rhythm, we endure.

A smile shared, a hand extended,
With every act, our fears are mended.
Harmony in the smallest deed,
A gentle touch, a simple need.

Together we create a song,
In a world where we belong.
With each note, compassion grows,
In every heart, the kindness flows.

The melody of love resounds,
In every corner, it surrounds.
In laughter, tears, and shared embrace,
A timeless dance we interlace.

The rhythm moves from heart to heart,
Uniting souls, we play our part.
With every step, we rise above,
In the sweet cadence of our love.

Stumbling on Shared Smiles

In the park where sunlight streams,
We find joy in gentle dreams.
Stumbling on laughter, a simple bliss,
In the moments we can't miss.

Eyes connect, the world stands still,
In this space, we share our will.
A grin exchanged, a secret glance,
Life's beauty in our chance dance.

Even whispered words can spark,
Our hearts ignited in the dark.
With every stumble, grace appears,
Shared smiles wash away our fears.

We walk the path, hand in hand,
Navigating this vast land.
Together we face all life's trials,
Finding joy in shared smiles.

As twilight falls and day does end,
With all my heart, I call you friend.
Through every stumble, laughs and trials,
We cherish each of our shared smiles.

Footpaths of the Heart

Winding trails through whispers soft,
Every step a gentle thought.
Memories dance in shadows light,
Footprints left, a love ignites.

Silent echoes in the glade,
Every smile, a secret made.
Hand in hand, we trace the lines,
In the heart where truth aligns.

Through the trees the sunlight streams,
We walk together, woven dreams.
In the branches, stories bloom,
Footpaths carve away the gloom.

Fields of wildflowers sway,
With each moment, joy will play.
Whispers weave a tapestry,
Of life and love, eternally.

So let us roam, forever free,
Where the heart beats joyfully.
In the journey, hand in hand,
Footpaths lead through love's vast land.

Sails Set with Kindred Winds

On the sea where dreams unfold,
Our sails are set, bright and bold.
Kindred winds guide us away,
Beneath the sun's warm golden ray.

Waves of laughter, whispers sweet,
Together, our hearts skip a beat.
Navigating through joy, through tears,
With every sail, we conquer fears.

Stars above, our guiding lights,
In the dark of lonely nights.
Side by side, we face the storm,
Braving winds, our love is warm.

In the harbor, dreams alight,
Anchored close, holding tight.
With each tide, our spirits soar,
Together, we can face much more.

As long as we have hearts to steer,
The horizon's promise draws near.
With kindred winds, so gently born,
We'll sail forever, hearts reborn.

The Little Things That Bind

A gentle touch, a warm embrace,
In fleeting moments, we find grace.
Soft-spoken words that heal the soul,
In simple gestures, we feel whole.

Laughter shared over cups of tea,
Quiet hours where we feel free.
In the details of everyday,
Love blossoms in a tender way.

Notes left hidden, sweet surprise,
In small acts, our love complies.
A smile exchanged, a fleeting glance,
In every heartbeat, there's a chance.

Through tangled paths of life we weave,
The little things teach us to believe.
In the chaos, we find our peace,
A bond that grows, will never cease.

So let us cherish, let us take,
The tiny moments that we make.
For in these threads, our hearts align,
It's here we find, love's great design.

Shared Dreams in the Night Sky

Beneath the stars, our visions merge,
In whispered dreams, we feel the surge.
Constellations tell our tale,
In moonlit hours, we set our sail.

With every twinkle, hopes arise,
In the silence, hearts comprise.
Wishing on the shooting stars,
Together bound, no distance far.

As night unfolds its velvet cloak,
We share the dreams that softly spoke.
Hand in hand, through dark we roam,
In each other, we find home.

Dreams shared in the cool of night,
Illuminated by starlit light.
In every moment, warmth we feel,
Connected souls, our love is real.

So look above, let visions fly,
In shared dreams, we touch the sky.
Together we'll chase the dawn,
As morning breaks, a love reborn.

Milton Keynes UK
Ingram Content Group UK Ltd.
UKHW022003131124
451149UK00013B/996